Budgeting

Money and Me

Budgeting

by
Christina J. Moose

Rourke Publications, Inc.
Vero Beach, FL 32964

To Dad and Mom,
who got smarter as their kids got older

————————

Photo on page 2 by Tony Cuevas.

Produced by Salem Press, Inc.

Copyright © 1997, by Rourke Publications, Inc.
All rights in this book are reserved. No part of this work may be used or reproduced in any manner whatsoever or transmitted in any form or by any means, electronic or mechanical, including photocopy, recording, or any information storage and retrieval system, without written permission from the copyright owner except in the case of brief quotations embodied in critical articles and reviews. For information address the publisher, Rourke Publications, Inc., P.O. Box 3328, Vero Beach, Florida 32964.

∞ The paper used in these volumes conforms to the American National Standard for Permanence of Paper for Printed Library Materials, Z39.48-1984.

Library of Congress Cataloging-in-Publication Data
Moose, Christina J., 1952-
    Budgeting / by Christina J. Moose.
        p.   cm. — (Money and me)
    Includes bibliographical references and index.
    Summary: Explains the concept of a budget and how individuals, groups, and even governments need to plan to make the best use of their money.
    ISBN 0-86625-609-1
    1. Children—Finance, Personal—Juvenile literature. [1. Finance, Personal.
2. Budget.] I. Title. II. Series.
HG179.M619   1997
640'.4—dc21
                                                                97-6366
                                                                    CIP
                                                                    AC

First Printing

PRINTED IN THE UNITED STATES OF AMERICA

Contents

Making Choices

> *It was a mystery to Sarah. How did her best friend do it? Mandy had shown up at school wearing a new sweater that Sarah had been craving for months. It wasn't Mandy's birthday, and with four children her parents weren't rich. Mandy got only $20 allowance per week. That had to cover bus fare, school lunches, pet food, gifts for friends, club dues, after-school snacks, and any movies she wanted to see. Not much for a busy seventh-grader these days! Sarah got $25 per week, yet she never seemed to have enough to buy herself such luxuries. How **did** Mandy do it?*

Some children seem to have "all the luck." They wear the coolest clothes, they have video games—some even have their own CD player. There are so many things to buy. No one can have them all, but some have more than others. Why?

Where Do Young People Get Money?

Children and young adults can get money several ways: gifts from grandparents, selling fruit from the backyard, or earning money. Baby-sitting, mowing other people's lawns, and taking care of other people's pets are a few ways young people earn money.

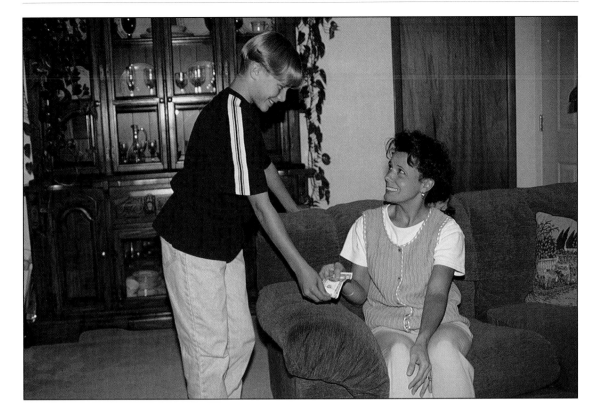

Children also get money from their parents. Some families are better off than others. A few parents spoil their children and give them whatever they want without making them work for it. Some parents work hard to give their children the basics—maybe just bus fare and a bag lunch for the day.

Children often get an allowance from their parents, usually once a week. (James L. Shaffer)

The luckiest children are like Mandy and Sarah. Their parents are not poor, but they aren't rich either. Most of these parents give their children some sort of allowance. An *allowance* is a set amount of money that parents give to their children, usually once a week. Parents often make it a rule that their children must use part of their allowance for things like bus fare and school lunches.

Mandy got $20 per week. She had to use some of that to buy lunch, pay for the bus, and feed her cat Slasher. She also belonged to the Girl Scouts and used her allowance to pay the dues of $1.50 per meeting. Finally, she had to use her allowance for

church donations and gifts. That was the deal
Mandy had with her parents.

Like Mandy, Sarah got an allowance. Hers
was much more: $25 per week, in fact. Part of it
also went for lunches, bus fare, food for her dog
Tramp, and gifts, but Sarah's parents paid for
Sarah's hip-hop dance lessons. Even so, it seemed
to Sarah that her allowance didn't go much farther
than Mandy's.

Then why are youngsters like Mandy and
Sarah so lucky? Because they can *decide* what to
do with any leftover money. Sarah and Mandy
had to spend part of their allowance on *needs* like
bus fare, school lunches, and pet food, but when
they had finished paying for these needs, they still
had some money left over. Their parents told them
that the leftover money was for things they *wanted*.
Mandy's and Sarah's parents were using an
allowance to teach their children about *money
management*.

**Money Management =
Deciding How to Spend Your Money**

So What Do You Really Want?

After Sarah saw her best friend wearing that
new sweater, she asked Mandy where she got the
money to buy it. Mandy told Sarah something
shocking: "I got the money from my savings."
Sarah couldn't believe it: "Yeah, sure! You only get
$20 allowance a week. That top cost $75 on sale!"
Still, Mandy swore that the money was her own.
Sarah saw that Mandy meant what she said, so she
asked the question that had been on her mind all
along: "How did you do it?"

"Well, if you really want to know, I made a *big*
decision," Mandy said. "What do you mean?" Sarah
asked. Mandy replied, somewhat mysteriously, "I

decided what it was I *really* wanted, and after that it was easy."

"Oh, if that's all, I should have no problem," said Sarah. "I know exactly what I want: roller blades, the new Toni Braxton CD, horseback riding lessons, season tickets for the Kings, that really cool hip-hop outfit at Dance World. . . ."

"Hold on a minute!" Mandy interrupted. "I didn't mean *everything* I wanted, just what I *really* wanted."

"But I *really want* all that stuff," Sarah insisted, "and besides, it doesn't matter, because I'll never have enough money to get any of it."

"Well then," Mandy countered, "how do you explain my sweater? At least I have *one* thing I really want—and I got it with my allowance. Don't you want one thing more than anything else?"

"World peace?" Sarah shrugged. She was beginning to become irritated with Mandy's obvious ability to control her money.

Children can also earn money by doing yardwork for neighbors. (Jim Whitmer)

"Look," Mandy explained. "Remember when you and Andrea and Mando went bowling last week after school? I said I couldn't go, remember? Later, when the group went to the movies and Burger Barn Saturday afternoon, I was baby-sitting, remember?"

"You *have* been sort of anti-social lately," Sarah sniffed, but she got the message. "You mean you were saving for the sweater, right?"

"Now you're getting the idea. By the way, we biked around the park for free on Sunday, so I haven't really been anti-social." Mandy wanted Sarah to know that she was still part of the crowd. "Besides, I had to make a *choice*. I really wanted that sweater. So my folks helped me."

"They gave you more money!" Sarah had suspected as much.

"No. They helped me make a *plan*. We wrote down all the money I had, and all the things I had to spend it on. Then we talked about what to do with the leftover money."

Sarah still wasn't convinced. "How can you have 'leftover money' when they give you only $20 a week?" She was beginning to wonder how she could find leftover money from her $25 per week.

"Because I found out that I spend money two ways: for things I *need*, and for things I *want*. Mom and Dad don't make me buy all the things I need, just some, so it turns out that I have more money to spend on *wants* than I thought!"

A Spending Plan

Mandy did not know the word for it, but she and her parents had made a *budget*. A budget is nothing more than a spending plan. A budget lets you decide what to do with your money *before* you spend it. That way, you know where your money is going: wherever *you* want it to go. Mandy had

Money is always spent on "needs," like food and household supplies, first.
(James L. Shaffer)

used her spending plan as a map to get from "no sweater" to "cool sweater." Here's how she did it.

Two Types of Spending

As Mandy had learned and as Sarah began to realize, people spend money in two ways:

- **Needs:** All of us have things we must buy, no matter what, called *needs*: food, a place to live, medicine when we are sick, and a way to get around, whether on a bike or on a bus. Money always goes to needs *first*. If no money is left over, then we must find ways of earning more money or ways of buying our needs with less money.

- **Wants:** Most of us, like Sarah, want lots of things that we do not really need in order to live. Children want things like cool clothes, games, sports equipment, movies, and snacks after school. Parents want things like a second

When you have paid for all your "needs," you can spend some of your "leftover money" on "wants," like a hot dog.
(James L. Shaffer)

car, a new home, and a family vacation. If there is any money left over after *needs*, we can spend it on *wants*.

Where Does the Money Go?

The first step to making a spending plan is to figure out how you spend your money right now. That means making a *spending record*. Before Mandy could plan the money for her sweater, she had to find out what was happening to the $20 her parents gave her every week. So for several weeks she wrote down everything she got and everything she spent.

After only two weeks, Mandy was beginning to learn a lot from her spending record. First, she *needed* to spend money on bus fare, lunch, pet food, church donations, and Girl Scout dues (or quit the Scouts). She also thought it was important to send cards and gifts to her family and friends, though she decided she might spend less money and more time making them herself. Everything else was things she *wanted* for herself but didn't really need.

Looking at her record, Mandy saw that she had very little at the end of each week. The week she baby-sat at the Andersons she had much more than her regular $20 allowance, but by the end of the week she had only fifty cents. It seemed as if she spent the money as soon as she had it.

Mandy began to wonder. She had wanted that cool sweater for weeks, but she thought she would never be able to afford it. Now she began to look at the "wants" she had been buying.

Mandy was amazed. The things she didn't really need cost $20.50 — more than a whole week's allowance, and a big chunk of the cost of that sweater! She could have made a card for Aunt Melinda using her paint supplies at home, and her aunt would have liked it better. She would have been happy to trade her other purchases for

MANDY'S SPENDING RECORD

WEEK #1
Money I got:

Money left over from last week	$ 0.00
Allowance	20.00
Total I got	**20.00**

Money I spent:

Bus to and from school (5 days @ $1 per day) . .	$ 5.00
Lunch (5 days @ $1.50 per day)	7.50
Slasher's food for week	2.00
Church donation	1.00
Girl Scout dues	1.50
Birthday card for Aunt Melinda	1.25
Large cola at Burger Barn after school Friday . .	1.00
Total I spent	**$19.25**

Total I got	$20.00
Minus total I spent	−19.25
Money left over	**$ 0.75**

WEEK #2
Money I got:

Left over from last week	$ 0.75
Allowance	20.00
Birthday gift from Grandma	5.00
Baby-sitting for the Andersons	10.00
Total I got	**$35.75**

Money I spent:

Bus to and from school (5 days @ $1 per day) . .	$ 5.00
Lunch (5 days @ $1.50 per day)	7.50
Slasher's food for week	2.00
Church donation	1.00
Girl Scout dues	1.50
Celine Dion CD	12.00
Bowling with Mando, Sarah, and Andrea	3.25
Hamburger and fries at bowling alley	3.00
Total I spent	**$35.25**

Total I got	$35.75
Minus total I spent	−35.25
Money left over	**$ 0.50**

```
┌─────────────────────────────────────────────────────────┐
│ ┌───────────────────────────────────────────────────────┐ │
│ │            MANDY'S "WANTS" SPENDING                    │ │
│ ├───────────────────────────────────────────────────────┤ │
│ │ WEEK #1                                               │ │
│ │ Birthday card for Aunt Melinda . . . . . . . .  $1.25 │ │
│ │ Large cola at Burger Barn after school Friday . .  1.00 │ │
│ │                                                       │ │
│ │ WEEK #2                                               │ │
│ │ Celine Dion CD . . . . . . . . . . . . . . . . . $12.00 │ │
│ │ Bowling with Mando, Sarah, and Andrea . . . .   3.25 │ │
│ │ Hamburger and fries at bowling alley . . . . . .  3.00 │ │
│ │      Total "wants" spending . . . . . . . . . . $20.50 │ │
│ └───────────────────────────────────────────────────────┘ │
└─────────────────────────────────────────────────────────┘
```

the sweater, if only she had thought about it ahead of time. Mandy was finally ready to make a plan.

Building the Plan

Making a spending record had already taught Mandy a lot about making a spending plan. Only this time, Mandy would not list things she had already bought. Instead, she would list those things she *planned* to buy in the future.

Step 1: List your income. First, Mandy knew she had to list all the money she got from allowance, baby-sitting, and gifts. Her dad told her that this money is called income. *Income* is the total money that "comes in" to you. Here's where people get income:

- **Allowance:** This is the main source of income for children. When you grow up, you probably will not have an allowance. Instead, most of your money will come from earnings.
- **Earnings:** Any money you get for working is *earned income*, or earnings. Earned income includes money you get for doing odd jobs for other people, such as baby-sitting or car-washing. The government taxes earned income, but most children under fourteen do not earn enough to get taxed. If you earn money at a job, you must check with your parents about taxes.

If you include savings in your budget, you can buy something expensive that you would like to have. (Jim Whitmer)

- **Gifts:** Any money someone gives you without expecting anything in return is a gift. Birthday money is a good example. Most gift money is not taxed by the government unless it is a very, *very* large amount, so children usually don't need to worry about taxes on gifts.
- **Investment income:** This can be money you get for *lending* your own money to someone

else (like a bank). Such money is called *interest*.
You can also get money if you *buy* a part of a
company called a *share*. If the company makes
lots of money, its shares can become more
valuable. Sometimes, when the company does
well, it will pay its shareholders money called
dividends. You can also sell shares to someone
for more money than you paid in the first
place—but watch out. Sometimes a company
doesn't make as much money as everyone
expected. Then you can lose money on your
investment. Another thing to remember:
Investment income gets taxed, too.

Step 2: List your expenses. Second, Mandy
had to list the things she would buy with her
money. These are called *expenses*, or sometimes
expenditures. Mandy already knew the needs she
had to purchase every week. These needs are called
fixed expenditures, because usually they are the same
from week to week and their cost is the same, too.

Step 3: Subtract to find disposable income.
Finally, Mandy knew that she would probably
spend money on *wants*, but these wants would be
different every week. These expenses are called
discretionary expenditures. ("Discretionary" just
means "according to what you want.") This was
Mandy's favorite part of the spending plan—the
place where she would find money for clothes
and other things she wanted.

Mandy also knew that she had to pay for her
needs, or fixed expenditures, before she could
use any "leftover money" for her discretionary
expenditures. Any leftover money is called
disposable income.

> **Income – Expenditures for Needs =**
> **Disposable Income**

Mandy's Spending Plan

Mandy's first spending plan looked a lot like her spending record, but she made it so it would fit most typical weeks.

When Mandy saw that only $3.00 of disposable income was left over for her wants, she was a little disappointed. Then she remembered that the Andersons had asked her if she could baby-sit for them on Fridays for the next several weeks. Mandy hated to give up her Friday evenings, so she had said no at first. Now she had second thoughts. She picked up the telephone to call Mrs. Anderson. Did she still need a baby-sitter for Fridays? The answer was yes, and Mandy knew she could add ten dollars to the "Income" section of her weekly budget.

Suddenly Mandy understood why budgeting for *next week* was much better than

MANDY'S WEEKLY SPENDING PLAN: ROUGH DRAFT	
INCOME:	
Money left over from last week	$ 0.00
Allowance	20.00
Earnings (baby-sitting for the Andersons)	0.00
Gifts	0.00
Investments	0.00
Total income	**$20.00**
EXPENSES:	
Bus to and from school (5 days @ $1 per day) . .	$ 5.00
Lunch (5 days @ $1.50 per day)	7.50
Slasher's food for week	2.00
Church donation	1.00
Girl Scout dues	1.50
Total expenditures	**$17.00**
DISPOSABLE INCOME (LEFTOVER MONEY):	
Total income	$ 20.00
Minus total expenditures	–17.00
Equals disposable income	**$3.00**

MANDY'S WEEKLY SPENDING PLAN: FINAL DRAFT

INCOME:

Money left over from last week	$ 0.00
Allowance	20.00
Earnings (baby-sitting for the Andersons)	10.00
Gifts	0.00
Investments	0.00
Total income	**$30.00**

EXPENSES:

Bus to and from school (5 days @ $1 per day) . .	$ 5.00
Lunch (5 days @ $1.50 per day)	7.50
Slasher's food for week	2.00
Church donation	1.00
Girl Scout dues	1.50
Total expenses	**$17.00**

DISPOSABLE INCOME:

Total income	$ 30.00
Minus total expenses	–17.00
Equals disposable income	**$13.00**

DISCRETIONARY EXPENDITURES:

Savings for sweater	$ 9.00
Photo album for Sarah	
(hand-decorated by Mandy)	3.00
"Mad" money (for snacks and hanging out) . . .	1.00
Total discretionary expenditures	**$13.00**

---

simply recording what she spent *last week*: The future has not happened yet. She could adjust her plan to make it possible to buy her wants. Now she could look forward to having $13 (not just $3) at the end of the week.

What would she do with it?

Budgeting for a Goal

Mandy was about to make the "big decision" she had described to Sarah. Believe it or not, this proved to be the hardest part of the budgeting process: What would she do with her disposable income?

She sure wanted that sweater, but $13 was barely enough to buy a CD for Sarah's birthday. Also, Mandy's friends were planning to go to Burger Barn after school on Friday, and Mandy wanted to go, too. She would need money for at least a soft drink.

It began to seem hopeless until she made the "big decision": "I *really want* that sweater," she thought. Mandy decided to *save* at least some of the money for the sweater. She also decided that she would skip Fridays at Burger Barn, since she had to get ready to baby-sit anyway. Instead, she would try to meet with her friends for free activities, like biking or watching music videos.

**Savings = Money You Keep for
Something You Want in the Future**

The final draft of Mandy's weekly spending plan had a section called "Discretionary Expenditures" with the line "Savings for sweater." She figured that she could set aside nine dollars for the sweater and still use a *little* for fun. In other words, Mandy had decided to "spend" some of her disposable income on her sweater. Even though she wouldn't actually get the sweater until she had all the money, in a way she was still spending her money on something she wanted.

Looking Ahead

In eight weeks, Mandy had her new sweater. It was the first expensive thing she had ever purchased. She was especially proud to wear it because she had bought it with her own money. She began to look ahead to new goals she could set for herself.

At the moment, though, Mandy could not decide on anything really special. Oh, there were all sorts of things that she might buy, but nothing like that sweater. Still, she liked the idea of having some money *in case* she needed or wanted to spend it, so she decided to keep the baby-sitting job as long as the Andersons needed her help.

One evening at the dinner table, she decided to ask her parents what they thought she should do with the money she was saving. Her mom and dad looked at each other and smiled. Was Mandy ready for the next step?

A Family Budget

Mandy had learned about using a budget to reach a short-term goal: buying her sweater. Yes, eight weeks had seemed like a long time, but any period less than a year is usually called a "short term." Now it was time to learn something about long-term goals.

A *long-term budget* is one that plans spending for a year or more. Long-term budgets also help in planning for *big* goals—goals that take more than a year to reach. For children, long-term goals include things like buying a bicycle. For teenagers, buying a car and helping pay for college are long-term goals. Parents have many long-term goals, like buying a house, sending their children to college, and saving money for retirement.

"You know," Mandy's dad said, "Mom and I were talking about how long it has been since the whole family did something *fun* together."

Like a vacation? Mandy wondered. "How about a ski trip?" she offered.

"Well," her mom hesitated, "first we need to see where it fits in the *family budget*."

"Oh . . . yeah." Mandy's excitement began to fizzle. She had two brothers—Bill, in sixth grade, and Mark, in ninth. There was always something her folks needed to buy for them: braces, eyeglasses, football uniforms. Her sister Samantha was a junior in high school and expected to start college soon. Mandy didn't know how much *that* cost, but she knew it was even more than braces.

"Hey, lighten up," her dad said, seeing her disappointed look. "You got your sweater, didn't you? At first you thought that was impossible. Maybe with a little thinking we can all figure out a way to take that ski vacation."

The next Saturday, Mandy's parents presented the family budget to Mandy, Samantha, Bill, and Mark. It looked a little like Mandy's weekly budget, but a lot longer. It had sections for "Income" and "Expenses," like Mandy's. Looking at the expenses, the children saw things none of

YEARLY BUDGET FOR MANDY'S FAMILY

INCOME:

Dad's salary	$32,000
Mom's salary	30,000
Samantha's part-time job	2,500
Investment income (interest + dividends)	1,000
Total	**$65,500**

EXPENSES:

Taxes:

Federal	$ 8,000
State	3,000
Property taxes, city/county fees	1,500
Car registrations and fees	300

Insurance:

Social Security and Medicare contributions	4,750
State disability insurance	250
Home insurance	900
Car insurance	2,000
Medical and dental insurance	1,500

Debt:

Home mortgage	7,000
Car payments	3,000
Credit cards	0
Charitable giving	2,000

Living expenses:

Utilities (gas, electricity, phone, water, trash)	2,000
Food and household supplies ($400/month)	4,800
Clothing and personal items	2,400
Car maintenance and gas (two cars)	2,000
Medical (medicines, doctor and dentist visits)	2,500
Children (allowances, school supplies, lessons)	4,000
Gifts for family/friends	1,000
Entertainment and recreation	1,000
Total expenses	**$53,900**

SAVINGS FOR NEEDS:

Children's college funds	$ 2,000
New roof	500
Retirement savings (401K, other)	7,000
Emergencies	2,000
Total savings for needs	**$11,500**

DISPOSABLE INCOME: Income – (Expenses + Savings) . . . . $ 100

*Parents can show
children how the
family budget works.*
(Jim Whitmer)

them had thought about, like taxes and insurance. Their folks had placed "Charitable Giving" in this section, too. They all agreed that it was important to set aside something for people who were not as lucky as they were.

The family budget also had sections Mandy didn't recognize: A big one was called "Living Expenses." Like fixed expenditures, *living expenses* are needs. Unlike fixed expenditures, however, living expenses can change from day to day, depending on prices and how good you are at finding bargains. There certainly were lots of them: food, clothing, gasoline, visits to the doctor, payments for the house and cars. Mandy looked at the clothing allowance and did some quick division: With six in the family, her part of the clothing budget was only $400 a year. No wonder her mom thought that her seventy-five-dollar sweater was expensive!

Finally, there was a new section called "Savings
for Needs." This was for long-term goals, like
college — not just for Samantha but for Mandy, Bill,
and Mark, too. Another thing was the roof, which
would have to be replaced in a few years. Mom
and Dad had even thought about the day when
they would be too old to work and would need
to live off their retirement savings. Boy, talk about

*Living expenses are
the things we must
buy from day to day—
and there are always
a lot of them!* (Jim
Whitmer)

looking ahead to long-term goals! It was hard enough for Mandy to think ahead to next week, let alone twenty years from now.

"Disposable Income" fell at the very bottom, with only $100 for the entire year. That didn't look too promising.

Save Something for Fun!

Suddenly, Mandy hated budgets. What was the use of having a spending plan if you couldn't *plan* for anything you really wanted? Budgets sure had a nasty habit of making everyone realize how many *needs* there are, and how little money there is for *wants*.

Luckily, Mandy's parents had remembered something important: Every month, they set aside some of their money — a small amount, but at least a little — for something called "Entertainment and Recreation."

"If you don't plan to treat yourself with something you want," her dad said, "your budget becomes your enemy. Make it your friend. That way you'll stick to it."

The family discussed what they would like to do with this part of their money. Together they decided to go for that ski vacation, until they learned it would cost a lot more than the $1,000 in "Entertainment and Recreation."

It seemed like the ski trip was out. Then Bill, Mark, Mandy, and Samantha realized something: They *really wanted* to go. They knew how much they wanted to go, because they started to think of all sorts of things they could do to make that trip a reality.

Finding a Way

"We need a vacation fund!" Bill and Mark insisted. They were stuck on the idea of snowboarding down the slopes, so they offered

A paper route is a way for boys and girls to earn extra money. (James L. Shaffer)

to contribute some of the money from their paper route.

Now that she had her sweater, Mandy could contribute money from her baby-sitting job. Samantha could afford only some of the money from her part-time job at Burger Barn. (She was using half of it for her college fund.) Luckily, Mom had just received a raise at her computer job, and she offered to put some of the extra income into the vacation fund. Dad said he could match Mom's amount.

Using Money to Make Money

To avoid the temptation to spend their vacation money on other things, Mandy's dad used the family's first installment to open a special account at the bank, called a *savings account*. That way, the money was separated from their other savings. Unless there was an emergency, they would use the money for their ski vacation.

There were two other reasons to keep their vacation money at the bank. First, money in a bank is insured by a government agency called the Federal Deposit Insurance Corporation, or FDIC for short. If the bank goes out of business, the FDIC pays your money back to you. That makes your money safe.

A second reason to open a savings account is that *deposits* (the money you put in) earn interest. *Interest* is an amount of money that a bank periodically adds to your account, to pay you for letting the bank use your money for other investments. (These investments make even more money for the bank.)

Sound Interesting?

Interest is paid as a percentage of the amount in your account. If you have $100 in a savings account that pays annual interest, and you do not *withdraw* (take out) any of that $100 during the year, the bank adds a certain percentage of the $100 to your account. At 2 percent, that's two dollars. At the end of the year, then, you would have $102. Two extra dollars may not seem like much, but it's more than you had at the beginning of the year.

When you earn interest on the *principal* (the original amount) *and* on the interest (the two dollars), that's called *compound interest*. Many banks pay compound interest.

COMPOUND INTEREST:
HOW MUCH CAN MY MONEY GROW?

Here's how your money would grow if you deposited $100 of birthday money (the *principal*) in an account that earned simple interest at an annual rate of 5 percent (the *rate*) for one year (the *period*). Here's the formula for math brains:

Principal + (Principal x Rate x Periods) = Future Value
$1,000 + ($100 x 5% x 1 year) = $1,050

If today is your eleventh birthday, and you leave that same $1,000 in that same account at the same rate, but *compound* interest, guess how much it will be worth when you turn twenty-one?

$1,629.00

You did not have to work for the extra money. Instead, your money "worked" for the compound interest. Happy birthday!

Most people don't earn much interest on the money they have in savings accounts, because the *rate* (the percentage of interest) is usually low. However, people can earn a higher rate of interest in several ways. One is to buy a CD. No, not a music CD. This CD means *certificate of deposit*.

A CD can cost more than it takes to open a savings account, often $1,000. Also, you must agree not to withdraw your money for a period of time—six months, one year, or even more. However, there's a reward for leaving your money alone in a CD account: At the end of the period, called the *maturity date*, the bank will pay you a higher rate of interest than it pays for savings accounts. Instead of 2 percent, for example, it might pay 5 percent.

Another way to "grow" money is to keep it in a *money market account*. Money market accounts also earn a higher rate of interest than savings accounts, sometimes even higher than a CD. You must usually have a lot of money to open a money market account, but you don't have to wait to take the money out, as you must with a CD.

Savings accounts, CDs, and money market accounts are three ways to lend your money and get paid you for it, with interest. Buying stocks and bonds is another way. All of these are different types of *investments*. Income from investments is taxable, so you have to think about that when you are budgeting.

Young people usually do not need to know much about investing and investment taxes. Still, the earlier they learn, the better off they will be as adults, because investments are usually necessary to meet long-term goals.

Keeping on Track

Mandy's family decided to "grow" their money to meet their vacation goal. With the $1,000 already budgeted for "Entertainment and Recreation," they bought a CD that paid a 5 percent rate of interest. At the same time, Mandy, her sister and brothers, and her mom and dad continued to deposit their contributions into the vacation account.

To keep the family's goal firmly in mind, Mandy and her mom taped an old poster of the Winter Olympics on the refrigerator door. The poster showed a gold-medal skier racing down a snowy slope, with pine trees on either side. At the bottom of the poster, Samantha stapled a big manila envelope where they put their vacation deposits. Once a week Mandy and her dad went to the bank to deposit the money in their vacation account.

It wasn't always easy, but after a while, making these "envelope deposits" became a habit. Everyone nearly forgot about it, in fact—except on those days when Dad or Mom would read their *bank statement*. This was a printed report from the bank showing how much money, including interest, was in the vacation account. The money kept growing, and that encouraged everyone to keep saving.

At the end of a year, they had all the money they had saved, the interest it had earned, *plus* a CD that was worth $50 more than what they had paid for it. Even after paying the taxes on this investment income, Mandy and her family had enough money to fly to Colorado for their ski vacation.

Instead, they decided to drive to the Sierras, closer to where they lived. They all agreed that the money they saved on airplane tickets could be spent on extra ski lessons and lift tickets. They even rented a condo with a fireplace and a view of the slopes!

CHAPTER 4

Group Budgets

Mandy had learned a lot about money and budgets in the last year. She knew that you can use a budget to plan how to spend your own money. That's called a *personal budget*. She had also learned about a more complicated kind of budget, for a group of people, called a family budget, or *group budget*.

Who Else Uses Budgets?

Many other groups use budgets to keep track of their money and to reach goals. Some of these groups include clubs, schools, churches, businesses, charities, and all kinds of governments. In fact, any organization that handles money has a budget—even banks!

Why all this budgeting? For one thing, many people belong to, or do business with, such organizations. In clubs, like the Scouts, members pay fees and dues so the club can buy supplies and go on field trips. In charitable organizations, people make donations so that those who need food and shelter can get them. No matter what the organization's purpose, it is important to keep track of all the money coming in (income) and going out (expenses), so that the people who

A family is one type of group that uses budgets. (James L. Shaffer)

contribute can be sure their money has gone where it should go.

Another reason that organizations budget is to plan how to spend their money in the future: to budget for goals, like Mandy's family did. Just like people, organizations must pay for their needs first. They must pay for taxes, insurance, and supplies. They must also pay the people who work for the organization. Some businesses offer to pay for their employees' medical insurance, too. There may be many different needs, depending on the organization.

With any "leftover money" the organization can do a wide range of things. What happens to this money depends on the organization's purpose and the desires of the people who belong to the organization. A budget must show that the leftover money is being used for the right reasons. Businesses need to show that they are making a profit, so they can pay their employees and their shareholders. Churches need to show that they are using the money for *nonprofit* reasons, because their purpose is to help others. Political parties need to show that their money is not being used to line some corrupt politician's pocket. They also need to prove they got the money legally, not as a bribe from some group that wants to control the politician.

The organization's budget shows both where the money comes from and how the money is being used. Organizations show their budgets to their members, to the government, and to shareholders to prove that the money is going where it is supposed to go.

Who Works with Budgets?

There are as many different types of people who work with budgets as there are organizations that use budgets. In fact, almost everyone works with a budget at some time during life, even if it's only a

---

HOW BUSINESSES USE LEFTOVER MONEY

A business is one type of organization that uses a budget. Like families, businesses have fixed expenditures such as taxes and insurance. They must also pay *operating expenses*, such as rent and salaries. Any leftover money is called *profit*.

Businesses use their leftover money for purposes that the owners of the company agree will keep the business alive and growing. Some of these include:

- investing in new equipment, called *capital goods* or simply *capital*

- studying new ideas for making more money, called *research and development*

- hiring new workers and creating new jobs

- paying people called *stockholders* who have invested their money in the company; these payments are called *dividends*

personal budget. Most people will also have to deal with some kind of group budget, too.

There are even jobs that require people to work with budgets:

- **Accountant:** A person who helps a business organize and analyze the money it earns and spends in financial transactions. A *financial transaction* is any exchange of money between two parties for goods or services. Accountants help businesses *balance* their budgets. That is, they make sure that the amount of money coming in matches the amount of money going out for spending and savings. Accountants also help businesses plan and prepare their taxes. A *certified public accountant* (CPA for short) is a person who has passed a government test to prove that he or she is qualified.
- **Bank teller:** The person at the bank who greets you at the window and helps you make deposits

All sorts of organizations use budgets, from businesses to school boards.
(James L. Shaffer)

into, or withdraw money from, your account. This person must verify that you have enough money in your account to make a withdrawal. Today, many bank tellers are being replaced by computers called *automated teller machines* (ATMs).

- **Bookkeeper:** A person who records the financial transactions of a company or other organization. These records are used to develop the company's budget. Bookkeepers must be very careful, and very accurate. Today, computer programs help bookkeepers do their job.
- **Chief financial officer (CFO):** The person at a company who is in charge of planning the business's financial goals and making sure it meets them. This is usually a very important and high-paying job.
- **Financial adviser:** A person who specializes in helping other people plan their budgets, invest their money, and reach their financial goals.

A teller must understand budgets and check to make sure you have enough money in your account to make a withdrawal. (James L. Shaffer)

- **Tax planner:** A person who understands the tax laws and helps others to plan their budgets to make sure that they do not pay too much, or too little, tax. Tax planners may also be lawyers or accountants.

These are only a few of the jobs that might interest you if you are good at math and like to work with numbers. Even if you aren't a math whiz, at some time in your life your boss will probably ask you to "stick to the budget." Better stick to that math homework!

Government Budgets

The biggest budgets are those for the biggest groups of people, like all the people who live and work in a city or a state or a nation. People who work pay many kinds of taxes to support all sorts of *governments*: local, state, and federal. These taxes pay for hundreds of services and programs that we all enjoy, as well as some programs in which only certain people participate.

The people who work in government are elected and appointed to oversee the spending of our taxes. They have a special responsibility: They must make sure that they spend our tax money on things that we, the people, need and want. Whether at the city, state, or federal level, the job of government leaders who watch their part of our "tax budget" is very important.

Where Does the Government Get Money?

We have talked about taxes throughout this book. What, exactly, are they?

Taxes are fees imposed by governments to pay for public goods and services. A tax is levied as a certain percentage of a larger sum of money, like wages or the price of something you buy.

You've probably heard your parents talk about taxes. People usually complain about having to pay taxes because taxes take such a big chunk of their incomes. To get an idea, go back to Chapter 3 and look at the "Yearly Budget for Mandy's Family."

There are many kinds of taxes, but the ones most people really notice are the taxes taken out of their paychecks. These are federal income tax and state income tax. For example, income tax is *deducted from* (taken out of) your mom's paycheck as a percentage of her *gross* pay (that is, her pay before taxes). If her gross pay was $24,000 in 1995, she would have paid about $2,300 in federal income tax alone. She would have paid about $1,800 for Social Security and Medicare— contributions to social insurance programs that most people think of as taxes. State income tax depends on where you live. In California, where Mandy's family lived, it added up to about $275. After all these taxes and a few other deductions, Mandy's mom took home about $1,600 per month out of her gross pay of $2,000 per month.

Even if you don't get a paycheck, you've probably paid some taxes. Most state and local governments, for example, charge *sales tax*. When you buy something, whether it's a book or a bicycle, the total cost includes taxes. Sales tax varies from

At the end of 1995, Congress and President Bill Clinton could not agree on the United States' budget. The government had to stop working, and national museums were closed for a while. (AP/Wide World Photos)

state to state. In some states it's only 4 percent.
In other states it's nearly 9 percent. (Only a few
states have no sales tax.) The more you pay for
an item, the higher the sales tax. If you buy a
pair of sneakers for $100 in California, the tax
will be about $7.50—maybe a bit higher or lower,
depending on the city where you buy the sneakers.

If you own property, like a house, you also pay
property tax. If you own a business and have
employees, you must pay half of their Social
Security contributions.

What do taxes have to do with government
budgets? For governments, taxes are their main
source of income.

> **Government Income = Taxes + Borrowing**

Governments can also raise money by
borrowing. Issuing *bonds* is one way of borrowing.
Governments issue bonds in order to raise money
for things like roadways and school buildings.
The bond guarantees the *holder* (the person who
provides the funds in exchange for the bond) that,
at a certain date in the future, the government will
pay the holder the full value of the bond. This
value is greater than the amount of funds the
holder had to give the government for the bond.

Issuing a bond is really the same as taking
out a loan. It's a promise to pay back the money
borrowed, plus interest. Usually when a person
borrows money, he must promise to give the
person who lent the money something valuable,
like his house, in case he *defaults* on the loan (that
is, in case he cannot pay back the money). This
valuable thing is called *collateral*.

Governments do not offer collateral. They
trade on their good name only. Remember: The
"government" really means the "people." It's really

the people who have promised to pay back this loan. When the bond *matures* and it's time to pay the holder, the people will be paying back this loan, plus interest. How? With their taxes.

Government Spending

Even though people like to complain about paying taxes, the money taken out of their paychecks is spent for some good things. Cities put up stop signs, fix potholes, maintain the city parks, and pay police officers to fight crime. States fund the public schools and build highways and bridges, among other things.

The federal government maintains the armed forces to defend the nation in case of war. It issues Social Security and Medicare payments to help older people. It funds social programs that help poverty-stricken children or provide job training for adults. These are some of the things people buy with their tax dollars.

There is always a lot of argument about how the government spends its money and whether it is spending on needs or wants. Where there is little debate, however, is on government debt.

The National Debt

In the past, the United States federal government has borrowed money to meet some of its expenses. This borrowed amount is called the national debt. A *debt* is simply borrowed money that must be paid back. The U.S. government owes nearly five trillion dollars. That's $5,000,000,000,000.00!

How has this debt grown? It grows when the government spends more than it takes in. This type of spending is called *deficit spending*. The United States' budget has shown a deficit nearly every year since 1931. In the meantime, the debt has been growing. In fact, in New York City, an electric sign is counting the total amount the nation owes, second by second. The numbers are racing higher and higher as people watch.

Something else is growing, which makes the problem worse. In Chapter 2, you learned how you can make money "grow" by lending it to someone who will pay interest. When you are the borrower, you are the one who must pay the interest. The problem is, the longer it takes to repay the debt, the more the interest on that debt grows, and the more money you must pay back. Even worse, you must keep borrowing more and more to keep up your payments.

The government has been paying the interest on this public debt for a long time. The pie charts show how much this costs. In 1995, U.S. taxpayers paid $232 billion dollars in interest for the national debt. That is 15 percent of the total income of the U.S. government—a big piece of the pie. Because we have delayed paying our debt, the American people can spend only $85 out of every $100 of

The U.S. government's debt is growing second by second, as this sign in New York City shows. **(AP/Wide World Photos)**

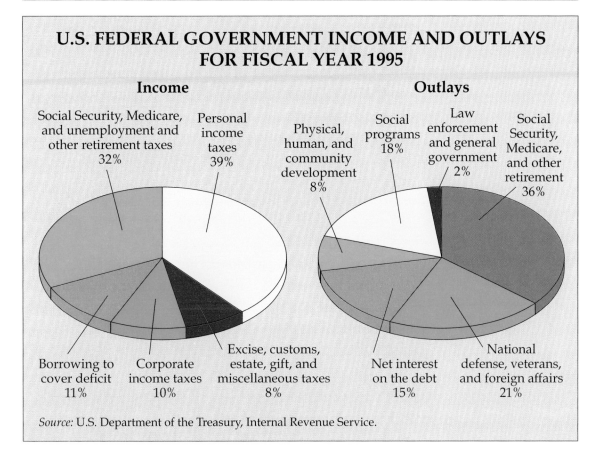

U.S. FEDERAL GOVERNMENT INCOME AND OUTLAYS FOR FISCAL YEAR 1995

Income

Social Security, Medicare, and unemployment and other retirement taxes 32%

Personal income taxes 39%

Borrowing to cover deficit 11%

Corporate income taxes 10%

Excise, customs, estate, gift, and miscellaneous taxes 8%

Outlays

Physical, human, and community development 8%

Social programs 18%

Law enforcement and general government 2%

Social Security, Medicare, and other retirement 36%

Net interest on the debt 15%

National defense, veterans, and foreign affairs 21%

Source: U.S. Department of the Treasury, Internal Revenue Service.

their taxes for needs and wants. That's like throwing away $15!

People disagree over how quickly to reduce the national debt to zero. Some argue that if we try to pay everything back too quickly, important social programs will suffer. Others say that if we continue to allow deficit spending, the interest payments will grow so high that our children will have to spend half their income — or more — on debt. Some people in Congress even want an amendment to the U.S. Constitution that would require a balanced budget every year.

Everyone agrees on one thing, though: The more this debt grows, the less there is to spend on needs and wants, and the poorer our nation will become.

These pie charts show the relative sizes of the major categories of federal income and outlays (expenses) for the fiscal year 1995.

Glossary

allowance: an amount of money that parents give to their children, usually once a week.

balanced budget: a budget in which income equals expenses plus savings.

budget: a spending plan that shows income, expenses, and savings.

collateral: a thing of value that a borrower promises to give a lender if the borrower fails to repay the loan.

compound interest: interest paid on both the original amount of a deposit (the principal) and any interest it earns.

debt: money borrowed that must be repaid.

deficit: the amount by which spending exceeds income.

deposit: money you put into a fund or an account.

discretionary expenditures: spending that is determined according to what one wants.

disposable income: income minus expenditures and savings for needs.

dividends: a portion of profits that a company gives its shareholders.

earnings: money paid for work completed or for time spent working.

expenditures: spending; amounts of money spent.

financial transaction: an exchange of money between two parties for goods or services.

fixed expenditures: types and amounts of spending that remain fairly constant over a period of time.

gift: money or something of value that someone gives you without expecting anything in return.

group budget: a spending plan for money that is generated and spent by more than one person.

income: the total money that "comes in," including earnings, gifts, and returns on investments.

interest: money paid for the privilege of borrowing or using someone else's money.

living expenses: spending for day-to-day needs.

long-term budget: a spending plan for a year or more.

money management: decisions about how you want to spend money.

needs: necessities for living, such as food, shelter, and medical care.

personal budget: a spending plan for one person.

principal: an original amount of money invested or borrowed, on which interest is earned or against which interest is charged.

rate: a percentage of interest.

sales tax: tax collected as a percentage of the cost of an item sold.

savings: money put away for a planned future expenditure.

savings account: a bank account that gathers interest; its main purpose is for saving money for a goal.

spending record: a list of all purchases and other spending made over a period of time.

taxes: fees that governments impose on citizens and others in order to provide public services.

wants: things purchased to provide pleasure.

withdraw: to take an amount of money out of a bank account.

Sources

Adler, David A. *Banks: Where the Money Is*. New York: Franklin Watts, 1985.

Berg, Adriane G. *Your Kids, Your Money*. Englewood Cliffs, N.J.: Prentice-Hall, 1985.

Berg, Adriane G., and Arthur Berg Bochner. *The Totally Awesome Money Book for Kids and Their Parents*. New York: Newmarket Press, 1993.

Berry, Joy. *Every Kid's Guide to Intelligent Spending*. Chicago: Children's Press, 1988.

Blue, Ron, and Judy Blue. *Money Matters for Parents and Their Kids*. Nashville, Tenn.: Thomas Nelson, 1988.

Blum, Laurie. *Free Money for College*. New York: Facts On File, 1993.

Cassidy, Daniel J., and Michael J. Alves. *The Scholarship Book*. Englewood Cliffs, N.J.: Prentice-Hall, 1990.

Drew, Bonny. *Fast Cash for Kids*. Hawthorne, N.J.: Career Press, 1991.

Drew, Bonny. *Moneyskills*. Hawthorne, N.J.: Career Press, 1992.

Dunnan, Nancy. *Banking*. Morristown, N.J.: Silver Burdette, 1990.

Faber, Doris. *Wall Street: A Story of Fortunes and Finance*. New York: Harper & Row, 1979.

Godfrey, Neale S., and Carolina Edwards. *Money Doesn't Grow on Trees: A Parent's Guide to Raising Financially Responsible Children*. New York: Simon & Schuster, 1994.

Kyte, Kathy S. *The Kids' Complete Guide to Money*. New York: Alfred A. Knopf, 1984.

McCee, Cynthia Ruiz, and Phillip C. McCee, Jr. *Cash for College*. New York: Hearst Books, 1993.

McDiarmid, Teena. *Making Money*. Milwaukee: Penworthy Publishing, 1988.

Otfinoski, Steve. *The Kid's Guide to Money: Earning It, Saving It, Spending It, Growing It, Sharing It.* New York: Scholastic Inc., 1996.

Schmitt, Lois. *Smart Spending.* New York: Scribner's, 1989.

Shanaman, Fred. *The First Official Money Making Book for Kids.* New York: Bantam Books, 1983.

Wallace, David. *How to Turn Lemons into Money: Money Basics.* Englewood Cliffs, N.J.: Prentice-Hall, 1984.

Weinstein, Grace W. *Children and Money.* New York: New American Library, 1985.

Weinstein, Grace W. *Money of Your Own.* New York: E. P. Dutton, 1977.

Index